THE POWER OF SHUT UP GRACE

7 Key Principles to Change Your Life Forever by Keeping Your Mouth Shut

Tonita Smith

THE POWER OF SHUT UP GRACE

DEDICATION

I would first like to thank God who is the author and finisher of my story. Without God on my side none of this would be happening. This book marks the completion of a goal that I've had for many, many years. Next, I dedicate this book to my husband who believed in me when nobody else did. He continued to nag me saying when are you going to start writing your book? Then when I started writing he nagged me saying when are you going to finish your book? Well, honey here it is, all packaged up in print with love especially to you, my biggest supporter.

I have to thank my cousins Lasonya, Michelle, Kenya, Marlon, Torree, and Sheila. There's nothing like cousins. My best friend Carol Johnson who said, you have my permission to write about me, lol. To my girls, my supporters in the "fun crew" you all know who you are, and anyone else I may have failed to mention, please don't charge it to my heart. Last but not least my sister in Christ Estacy Porter, this woman pushed me when I didn't want to be pushed. I am so thankful for your wisdom and most of all your drive. A Special thanks to CPT Bobb Rouseau, you have no idea how much you blessed me by offering to publish my book; beyond that you became my book accountability partner.

Foreword

It's said that herbs have the ability to cure all root causes of disease while prescriptions are just temporary fixes for the symptoms.

"The Power of Shut-Up Grace" is the herb that will help you heal yourself before you self-destruct from taking the medicine of saying whatever you feel like saying for self-gratification. Hebrews 4:12 says, "the word of God is quick, and powerful, and sharper than any two-edged sword" and simply put, this book helps you understand how to use it on yourself so that you refrain from abusing it when dealing with others.

I have always admired Tonita for her humor, tenacity, and perseverance to overcome any obstacle and I always knew that she would do great things. Needless to say, when she asked me to write her foreward, I was truly honored. I took the time to thoroughly read "The Power of Shut-Up Grace" and after I closed the book, I was not only amazed by her transparency and 100% realness but I was blessed! It wasn't just the impartation that blessed me but it was the fact that I got the chance to see her transformation. We grew up together as children and I have first-hand knowledge of her struggles and her victories that have made her into the woman she is today.

Some of you may not know Tonita personally but you will feel like you do by the time you're finished reading. I can honestly say that you're in for a treat as she allows each of us a front row seat into her world, her past failures, her struggles, and again her triumphs. She takes what would seemingly be a basic principle of when and how to "shut-up", what to say, and when to say it to another level. She teaches us how to apply basic principles through obedience and sacrifice and reveals each blessing that came after doing so. The rule that silence is golden is often overlooked and underrated but Tonita brings it to the forefront with clarity and leaves you with the desire to try it for yourself. Each chapter includes real stories and testimonies that are very relatable and she not only gives instruction but she shows her personality and sense of humor, which will more than likely make you fall in love with her humble spirit. She does not sugarcoat her shortcomings and has no shame sharing the fact that she continues to fall short. "Shut-up grace" is an intentional and practiced lifestyle and not just a one-time experience.

Tonita even goes as far as to reveal how she dealt with the "mother in law from hell" and tells the story of how humility and love wins every time, even when you feel justified in "going off".

Personally, I learned a thing or two about wanting to have the last word and I only wish I had these principles to apply to my life a long time ago. This book would have helped me to understand that the battle was never mine to begin with and I would have avoided unnecessary lessons and detours.

I urge you to dive into the principles and the workbook provided to you while allowing your spirit to take you through the journey of the canal whereby Tonita has birthed out principles from her pain. God's transforming power turned her into a wise woman, loving wife, sensitive mother, and a giving servant. While you turn the pages of "The Power of Shut-Up Grace", know that it is her sincere hope that you too will experience a great turn around headed for some of the greatest days you've ever seen in your life.

Sincerely,

Torree Boyd aka Transparent Torree

Evangelist, Lifecoach, & Motivational Speaker

Table of Contents

Introduction

When I had the idea to write a book, I thought I wanted to write books for children but lo and behold here I am sharing the most valuable lesson I've learned from personal struggles and experiences. I believe everyone has a story inside of them! To me, a story is simply a unique set of circumstances and experiences that will lead each person to their destiny. God empowers us to learn from our tests so that he may be glorified through our testimonies. Learning when to keep my big mouth closed has presented many challenges and trust me, I've had my share of growing pains! I know I'm not the only one who has said something "*in the heat of the moment*" or sent a text, or an email, or even left a voicemail and wished they could take it back. Unfortunately, there's no return button once we speak something into the atmosphere. This is why it's so important to push your internal pause button before responding or reacting in certain situations. As a child, I never really had this struggle. I was raised in an era where adults gave you a look and you knew to "*shut-up*" or you knew what would come next. Keeping my mouth closed became my struggle as a young adult because I felt no one could give me the look. I felt that I could say exactly what was on my mind. I would go as far to pride myself in being able to respond quickly or having a comeback in a heated situation. I was the Queen of giving out a good tongue lashing whenever I felt someone trying to insult me and I had many trophies that I no longer care to display. I used to be happy to say, "Girl, I shut him/her down!"

I argued with the best of the best and never got anything resolved except the other person shutting down. Back then, this meant another victory. My experiences, circumstances, trials, and tribulations have taught me a thing or two and that's why I want to be a blessing to someone else that struggles with learning how to walk close enough with God and be delivered through obedience, conviction and discernment that guides us to know when to speak and when to be quiet. People need to understand and realize that there is a time to speak and a time to be silent. I love the phrase "Shut-up Grace" because it doesn't sound as harsh or rude as telling a person to shut-up. Back in the day I would say shut the F*** up. Whew! I thank God for deliverance. Now doesn't saying "*I'm just going to have shut-up grace right now*" sound so much better? Thank God for lessons and wisdom.

I'm not claiming to have it all together but after 40 years of life's beat downs and hard lessons, I would like to shed light and wisdom on the one thing we have so much power and control over; our words. The tongue is the smallest organ on the body but yet so mighty and so powerful.

Why is that? We will explore 7 areas in our lives that can have great impact on our destiny. Lord knows, I have to practice shut-up grace on a regular basis some days more times than others but I will never forget just how powerful my tongue is. Do you know how powerful YOUR tongue is? Let's find out together.

CHAPTER ONE

LESSON 1: TRUST IN GOD'S TIMING

I consider myself to be a very opinionated person however I will give you the benefit of the doubt before I totally weigh in on what I think of your character. Who am I to judge? Well if you're an opinionated person like me then I'm sure you can relate. I'd like to think that I give great advice, which usually prompts me to have something to say about almost any situation. I will admit that over the years, I have calmed down a lot with expressing my opinion. I have learned some hard lessons by opening my mouth and rushing to give my unsolicited opinion a time or two.

Let's just say I have hurt the feelings of others and my big opinions forced some people to isolate themselves from me. The lesson I learned behind that was to first ask, "Do you want me to just be a listening ear, or do you want my honest opinion?" My close friends and family know that if they say they want my honest opinion that's exactly what they will get and they may not always like what I have to say. I take pride in being a "*Non-Bandwagon Friend*" which means I will never agree with you if I think you are wrong or are potentially making a mistake. I will not sit back and watch you crash unless you ask me to stay out of your business. Then, I will say a prayer for you and allow you to walk off the cliff as I wait at the bottom to give you the comfort you will surely need.

Sometimes, people would call me with issues that I may not feel equipped to give advice on, it is in those moments that I would activate "Shut-up grace", listen, and pray. If I knew the situation before they called I would pray about it and ask God to give me the words that he would have me to witness to the person. My prayers are "*Lord use me as your messenger. If it is your will, remove me and what I think, and tell me exactly what you would have me to say to this person.*" Many times, he gave me the words I needed but the times that I didn't hear him speak to me; I would simply respond to the person seeking advice saying, "*I don't know what to say in this situation, but I will pray with you and for you, and I would recommend you be still until God tells you exactly what to do.*" The worst thing any of us can do is to move out of season. Lord, knows I have also learned a lot of hard lessons by moving on my own time as well.

For it is written, Ecclesiastes 3:1 "*To everything there is a season and a time to every purpose under the heaven.*" What we have to remember is that once words have been put into the universe you can't pull them back as if they were never said. You can think about it and apologize, but again the words have already been said and received. The impact can be devastating to the receiver and although they may forgive you, they may never forget what you said and how it made them feel. Remember timing is everything.

James 1:19 says, (KJV) "*Wherefore, my beloved brethren, let every man be swift to hear, slow to speak, slow to wrath:*"

This is why shut-up grace is so important! I can remember many heated arguments where my husband thought he was right about something. You couldn't tell him he wasn't right. Being right is very important to him and he actually takes pride in it. One thing I have learned in my marriage to this man is:

#1 Learn to pick my battles.

#2 Peace is far more important than winning.

#3 Practice shut-up grace even when you feel your comment is justified.

Don't get me wrong, this doesn't mean you should become a doormat and let people say anything they feel like saying to you while you sit back and say nothing. This means you are to use the wisdom that God has given you to know when to speak and when to shut-up. Many times it isn't about you anyway; it's about the test that you're going through. I promise you that if you pray for wisdom, conviction, and discernment, the Lord will tap you on your shoulder and you will know when you need to be quiet.

Do you know what's better than bailing gracefully out of a heated situation by choosing to remain silent due to obedience? The blessings you will receive are due to your obedience to choose God over your will. God's timing is always on time and you can take that to the bank. It's when we venture into doing what we prefer in our own time that things seem to fall apart or we fail to get the results we desired. God knows all things, sees all things, and controls all things. He gives us free will of choice but if we choose him and follow his plans for our lives, we will be much better off. Take it from a woman who has bumped her head more than a few times.

Testimony

Some time ago, I started practicing the art of holding in my true feelings whenever I faced a situation. I would say just enough so that I didn't over step my boundaries to the point of no return. I specifically began to practice this with my family and close friends. They knew I wasn't going to get on their "bandwagon" so I would give them a glimpse of my stance on the issue and withhold everything else I was really feeling with silence. This is primarily because I take no pleasure in hurting someone else's feelings.

I once had a former friend named Linda. Linda and I were friends for over 20 years and we became so close that we were almost like sisters. We always supported each other in different things. Linda was very insecure and I always knew this about her but I never allowed that flaw to affect our friendship. I try to meet people exactly where they are in their life and be the best friend I can be to them. I loved her.

Linda was the type of friend that asked a lot of questions, mostly very uncomfortable questions of me and anyone else she came into contact with. I heard many times from different people, why does she do that? Or is your friend crazy? Why does she ask so many crazy questions? I would answer by saying, "Oh she doesn't mean anything by that, that's just Linda".

Linda had another close friend that she shared her inner most feelings with. She would share with her friend when she was upset with me but would never say anything to me. Whenever she told her friend about why she was upset with me, I would find out by the very person she told. I would never know why Linda was upset and this became very frustrating for me. I would try to address her concerns and I also tried many times to make her feel comfortable about sharing things with me.

One day I guess Linda had about all she could take or maybe her other close friend convinced her to speak her mind to me; and that's exactly what she did. She called me to let me have it! She had finally mustered up the courage to let me know exactly what was on her mind and all the things that she had been holding back for so long. She called to tell me everything she had felt offended by that I said or did to her going back several years. I sat quietly and listened to everything she had to say without interrupting her. This was very challenging!

This was the first time she had ever shared her true feelings with me so I wanted to hear her out. I wanted her to get out every single word. When she was finished I said, "Wow! I never knew you were holding all those things against me all this time. I am feeling so crazy because I thought we were closer and I thought we were fine but all along you have been holding a grudge against me. As I listened, I thought about what I was going to say when she was done. I didn't pray. I just sat quietly. When she finished, I apologized for everything that I did to hurt her and said had I known she was offended, I would've apologized a long time ago. I acknowledged her feelings as well, because even though I felt misunderstood, I couldn't change how she had already perceived or received my words and actions. I told Linda I was relieved that she got all this off her chest because it was never my intention to hurt her feelings. Taking the time to actually listen to Linda told me that I was a horrible friend to her from her perspective. Listening to her without thinking of what I would say to her as a rebuttal allowed me to hear what her heart was saying. In turn, I heard mine too. The moment of silence brought so much clarity to our friendship and it was then that I knew just how to and whether I should move forward.

I finished expressing my sincere apology to Linda and then spoke for myself. I truthfully expressed to her that I realized I have never been needed so much in a friendship and it overwhelmed me. I thought I was meeting Linda exactly where she was in her life but I couldn't fulfill her expectation of me to constantly stroke her ego and build her self-esteem throughout our friendship. I worked hard to walk on eggshells and be super careful about every word I said because she always seemed to take offense with me, no matter how hard I tried.

I also expressed my disappointment of having to hear she had an issue with me from everyone else except her. To avoid throwing those she talked about me to under the bus, I would give her the chance to speak by asking if I said something that offends her. I believe our communication would've been much better if she would've shared with me and considered me the way I shared and considered her. Overall, I told Linda that based on everything she said to me, we should say goodbye and end the friendship at that moment because I couldn't imagine going through another 20 years being friends with someone who has been so much work. Friendships shouldn't feel like hard work all the time and since she felt I was always offending her, then she should feel the same sense of relief.

Although, I still think about Linda and I do wish her well, God has given me so much peace after ending that friendship. I still have love for Linda and I wish her nothing but the best and I still pray for her as well. I just learned from this experience that everyone is not meant to be in your life forever. Some people have expiration dates and are there for a season. We have to make peace with God's plans and be willing to move on in love and peace.

Some relationships can start out one way and end another. With time comes growth and change; unfortunately everyone's path doesn't progress at the same rate or speed. You have to be able to accept when a toxic relationship has reached its expiration. Will you drink milk that tastes and smells spoiled just because there's over a half of gallon left? You pour it out and you accept that you may have lost a few dollars but you gained the satisfaction of not having an upset stomach. The Lord is so good, that he will give us warning signs when it's time to let go and move on. Once you've prayed about ending a relationship you must trust God's timing and his response. It may not be the answer you want to hear, but acceptance will help you to move forward.

I also learned that it's not good to hold things inside for too long. Some things just need to be said and I knew when to speak and what to say the moment I remained quiet while listening to Linda. Normally, I would've cut her off and let her and anyone else "have it" but I allowed the Lord to lead me in my silence and there was a greater outcome for me and for Linda. Remember to pray and ask God for the right timing and the guidance on what to say and how to say it. If you do this, I guarantee the outcome will be so much better.

Meditate on this scripture: Ecclesiastes 3:1 "*To every thing there is a season, and a time to every purpose under the heaven:*"

Workbook Pages 1-2

1. Have you ever been in a friendship or relationship that was very draining or overwhelming?

If so, how did you handle things? If you felt you could've handled things better, I want you to write 3 things you could've done to please God by making the situation better.

A.

B.

C.

2. Do you pray for your friends or the relationships that you're currently involved with?

3. Write down 3 ways you handle conflict:

A.

B.

C.

4. Write down 3 situations where you could've practiced shut-up grace and things could've gone in a more positive direction.

A.

B.

C.

5. Lastly, write down 3 things you would like God to help you to improve within yourself for better communication with others.

A.

B.

C.

Write down prayer requests that you want to petition God on someone else's behalf.

CHAPTER TWO

Lesson 2: The Birth of Shut-Up Grace

"Stop looking at the situation; keep your eyes on God"

I learned the valuable importance of shut-up grace in my first marriage but who knew that it was all in preparation for my 3rd. Yes, I said my 3rd marriage. I am not ashamed to admit that I have been divorced 2 times. I am living proof that the third time is a charm but I'm not advocating for divorce or multiple marriages. Remember this is my story and I want to be very transparent with you. I grew up very fast being born to a teenage mother who passed away when I was only 2 years old. She was 16 years old. My mother died from a brain tumor and I never had the opportunity to know her. I have very few memories of her because I was so young. I was raised by my maternal-grandmother, aunts, uncles, stepmother, and my father. I grew up in a house with a lot of chaos and dysfunction but it was my life, my reality. I saw far too many things as a child, but today I am so thankful that I am not a product of my environment. If the devil had his way, I would be either strung out on drugs or an alcoholic. Alcoholism and drug addiction runs heavy in my family and I am grateful that I've never been addicted to either. I decided very young that I wanted a better life than what I was dealt. In many ways I was selfish, but was I really selfish just because I wanted more? I was a good student and worked very hard to have nice things that my grandmother wasn't able to provide. At 12 years old, my first job was at a neighborhood convenience store every day after school. I would save my money to buy school clothes and other things I needed but whatever my money couldn't pay for, my aunt would help me out or I bought clothes from boosters. I loved fashion and I was willing to go to stores and shoplift if I had to. Most of the time I had the money to pay the boosters half price for what I wanted instead of stealing it myself; I really wasn't a good thief. I was too scary which made me look suspicious. Instead, my big cousin would tell me to come with her and her friends and pick out what I wanted. This was the beginning of my life in the fast lane.

By the time I was 15 years old I was working at McDonald's and met a well-known drug dealer. In the beginning I wasn't physically attracted to him, but he drove a very nice car and I heard he had lots of money. I was very inexperienced when it came to men but I was nobody's dummy. I wasn't about to be a side chick or a fool for no man. He found an opportunity to talk to me every time I worked in the drive-thru. Eventually we exchanged phone numbers and begin to talk. During one of our conversations, he told me he had 3 kids and this was a major turn-off for me.

I told him I didn't think things would work between us and I stopped calling him or accepting his calls. He didn't feel the same way and continued trying to pursue me. After some time, he came to me and said he had found out that the twin boys that he was claiming ended up not being his children and that at that point; he only has a daughter.

I thought to myself, "*maybe I should give him a chance*" and from the moment I did, he immediately started doing things for me financially and in turn, I equated his gifts with affection. The more he bought or the more

connection with the Lord. I would often find myself praying throughout my day no matter where I was or what I was doing. I would usually be the person most likely asked to lead prayer or start the conversations in our group. The more and more I did this, the bolder and more confident I became in God's word and understanding of his will for my life.

I began to see myself as an Evangelist. I would offer prayers and advice to anyone who chose to share their issues with me. I studied God's word and began to apply his teachings to my everyday life. Although I was never active on any ministries or committees in the church, I felt a stronger desire to reach people outside the walls of the traditional church setting.

I shared my idea with my cousin who is a hairstylist and we all know that women seem to trust their hairstylist and become comfortable enough to share their deep dark secrets. I suggested to my cousin that she should start praying while shampooing or styling her customer's hair so that God would work on them from the inside out. She said she would and that she'd specifically pray for a renewed mind and a cleansed heart. My cousin said sometimes the drama would be so thick she would have to wear ear buds to listen to gospel music; afraid that their junk would get into her spirit and cause destruction in her.

We decided that we would host an event to win souls by inviting any of her unsaved customers, our family, and friends. We were on a mission for the Lord! At this time, the sermon "No More Sheets" by Evangelist Juanita Bynum was out and very popular.

There were so many women, in our close circle, having issues with men and sleeping around and we felt that this specific message would be perfect to speak to their hearts. We planned to play the sermon and each woman involved in our ministry would share their personal testimony and tell why and what happened to make them decide to give their lives to Christ. We asked our Pastor to come at the end along with his wife to offer salvation to any woman that made the decision to accept Christ as their Lord and Savior. We purchased certificates to handout to commemorate that date that they were Born Again. This event was a huge success and we had already told ourselves that even if one woman accepted salvation on that day then it would be a success. I am proud to say that 7 women accepted salvation at that event. This was the just the beginning of us setting out to make God proud.

After the event, we started being asked by several men, why our ministry was only catering to women? They wanted to join us and felt that men needed salvation just as much as the woman if not more since man is given the charge to be the head of the household. We discussed it among the group and quickly realized that they were absolutely correct. We didn't realize the limits we had placed on God's power by restricting our ministry and guest list to women only.

This was the beginning of our expanded ministry of men and women which then led to the name change, "*Sister to Brother Outreach Ministry*".

We continued to meet, grow, and be on fire for the Lord. We would meet and discuss ways to reach more people and began planning for our next event.

One day God gave me the idea to write a play. It wasn't a Tyler Perry Play, but more on a scale of a high school musical play without the music. The play was called "*Time Waits for No One*". I began writing the play as instructed by the Lord and he started giving me characters and exactly who should play which character. I had this 25 page play written within 2 weeks. I couldn't believe it myself and it was actually pretty good. I presented my idea to the group at one of our prayer sessions and because I had already completed it, I was able to tell everyone about their character and their roles. Keep in mind none of us had any acting experience and I had no experience as a playwrighter or anything else for that matter. Do you know that when God gives you an assignment he will provide you with a roadmap? He will open doors and give you favor and all you have to do is answer to the call and get to work.

"*Favor isn't fair but it's necessary,*" ~Bishop Calvin Scott.

The scripture says: Faith without works is dead" These are true words to live by. As things begin to unfold, our prayer sessions expanded to rehearsals for the play. My cousin and I decided to have a meeting with our Pastor at the time to ask permission to have a Special Soul Winning Service in which we would have a guest speaker; an ex-drug dealer who had been delivered would share his testimony. It was at this event that we would perform our play.

Our play was a success and more than that, our guest speaker's testimony was so powerful that I believe about 20 people went to the altar to accept salvation. God had showed up and showed out!

One day, at one of our prayer meetings, I was discussing an issue I was having in my marriage with one of the sisters. I was explaining to her that my husband was always yelling at me whenever we would disagree and how I would yell back and we would have a screaming match, which left no resolution. On one hand, I am trying to live Christ-like in my everyday walk but on the other hand behind closed doors this man was pulling me out of my character. I didn't want to go back to the old Tonita. I didn't like that feeling, but I didn't know what else to do or how to fight. I explained that I prayed about it, but whenever he would start in on me, I always felt the need to defend myself with hurtful words. At the time I didn't recognize that I was being tested. She said, and I will never forget her words, "*Honey you need some shut-up grace.*" I looked at her like she was speaking another language. I was thinking do you know I have a tongue of fire? Didn't you see my trophies on display? Shut-up grace? I just knew I didn't hear her right! Was she telling me in a nice way that I needed to shut-up and let this man talk crazy to me? Absolutely not! She had the wrong one. I sat quiet for a moment to grasp exactly what she said as I was thinking of how I wanted to respond to her. "Shut-up grace…" I said. "What is that?" In a very gentle voice she began to break it down for me plus she probably saw my non-verbal facial expressions saying,

"Girl please you have me messed up." I was never good at hiding what I was thinking from my face.

She said shut-up grace is when you keep your mouth closed when the spirit of the enemy is present; in this way you are choosing God. "You see, it is spirits that use people to lash out in anger, there is a spirit that is using your husband." James 4:7 says, "*Submit yourselves therefore to God. Resist the devil, and he will flee from you.*" By keeping quiet, you are saying to God, "Father, this battle is not mine, but yours. I know if I say something it will come out all wrong so I will be silent and allow your spirit to overtake this battle and all that the enemy had planned, I give it to you. I know you never get it wrong so I will be quiet for you to speak instead of my flesh that wants to lash out in my own defense."

That was so powerful to me, I never forgot our conversation and I never forgot the meaning of "*Shut-up grace*" as explained by my sister in Christ. Over the years it has become a part of who I am. I sometimes post stats on Facebook or Instagram about the power of Shut-up Grace. I hash tag it #shutupgrace. I practice it all the time and still, sometimes I fail but I know that practice makes perfect. Now I'm asking you to ask yourself, what's more important? Pleasing God or winning the fight?

Remember if the Lord has already told us that the battle is not ours, it's his, then why do we focus on winning when we already have the victory? We have to walk in it, speak it, and believe it. This may take daily practice for some of us who have won a lot of trophies for cussing someone out and breaking them down with their words. As a part of spiritual maturity also comes responsibility to change or at least make attempts to make better choices. Who wants to go through the same test year after year only ending up in the same place? That's overwhelmingly exhausting.

Unfortunately, my husband chose to go back to the world. His cheating went to an all-time high and the disrespect was inexcusable. I had taken all I could take in that marriage and with God's permission, I chose to divorce and move forward.

With spiritual growth and responsibility comes a changed mindset. I no longer cared about staying with a man that didn't respect me enough to be faithful, just for the sake of our sons. I knew that my children and I would be fine and that God would provide for us. I learned lots of lessons that I otherwise would never have known, so even though the marriage came to an end, this was a road I had to travel as part of my journey to get to my final destination. If I kept my eyes on the situation and gave up on God just because my husband did, Lord only knows where I would be today.

Repeat this to yourself or out loud, "*I will trust God with everything, even during my storms, I will trust him and keep my eyes on my father and not the situation.*"

Proverbs 18:21 "*Death and life are in the power of the tongue and they that love it shall eat the fruit thereof.* (KJV).

Workbook page 1-2

1. How can you apply shut-up grace in your own life?

2. Can you think of a situation where you wish you could take back something you said to someone that you know was hurtful?

If you answered yes to question 2, write that person or persons name down on the line below

____

I challenge you to go to that person(s) whose name you wrote down or call them on the phone to apologize for what you said to them. I challenge you to ask them for forgiveness. Now, regardless of their response, when you're finished talking to them I want you to pray and ask God to forgive you, and then I want you to forgive yourself.

CHAPTER THREE

Lesson 3: You Have To Tame Your Tongue

It is written: (KJV) Proverbs 15:1 "*A soft answer turneth away wrath: but grievous words stirs up anger.*"

For those of us who have children, or can remember being a child, remember how your momma or your daddy would give you the "Look" and didn't have to say a word when you were acting up? With just one look, you knew you better shut your mouth or stop doing whatever it was that you were doing. That took discipline over time; rather it was from how your parents raised you or how you are raising your children. Most of us know what the "Look" means. It means if you say or do one more thing you are about to get your butt whooped. Whatever discipline techniques you parent your children with, or whatever discipline your parents used, it took discipline to submit to what was understood, right? We have to use the same type of discipline over time to get our tongue to submit because sometimes our mouths can get ahead of us.

How many times have you been in a situation and said something that you wish you wouldn't have said? How many times have you said to someone, I wish I would've kept my mouth closed then maybe all hell wouldn't be breaking loose? Ok, so this has only happened to me, lol.

Shut-up Grace is a form of art and discipline. I would consider it to be a verb because it is the act of doing something. Do you know how hard is to keep your mouth closed when you feel justified in speaking?? My God! This is a task but it takes thought and will power. I bet you can think right off the top of your head about a recent argument where you felt you were right and the other person was dead wrong. I bet you can think of lots of choice words to get them told and break them down.

I consider it to be an art because it is my belief that anything that requires you to think before acting is a form of discipline. It is so easy to open our mouths to make sounds or to speak when you're not spoken to. It is so easy to express our dislike or like for something. It is so easy to pass judgment or give our opinions even when nobody has asked for it. Communication is a form of art. Like listening, receiving, responding, it's all art. How loud is the sound of silence? Some people say that in silence, you can hear a pin drop or that it was so quiet and the tension was so thick you could cut it with a knife.

Have you ever walked into a noisy room and then all of a sudden when you entered everyone or everything became silent. How did that make you feel? I would guess quite uncomfortable, right?

Or how about you're arguing with someone or trying to get your point across and you are waiting for a response because you already have your next response in your head and you're just ready to pull the trigger, but then there's nothing; nothing but silence. The other person is exhibiting the art of silence and discipline. Silence is an action word that means the act of keeping quiet or not making a sound. But you see, it isn't because you can't make a sound; it is the conscious choice to not make a sound. Choosing to remain quiet when all hell is breaking loose around you takes discipline.

This is a skill that if practiced on a daily basis in a variety of situations you will become more aware of your power. I'm not suggesting you use it as power to get under someone else's skin or to use it in situations to get what you want like it's some kind of magic spell. Nor am I saying you should hold your words hostage. I'm merely suggesting you tap into the spirit realm and be very sensitive to God's voice, so much so that you hear him and feel his gentle tap on your shoulder to notion you to be still and to be quiet.

I challenge you to try using shut-up grace today or tomorrow or the next time you're in a situation that you realize that what you want to say may not come out right or may not be received in love.

Testimony

Those who know me now, but didn't know me before my deliverance, would never know that I use to be a "Curser." What's that? Well let me break it down for you. I used to curse so much that I stopped using the rest of my vocabulary because I liked how the curse words flowed off my tongue better. The words just seem to sound better or seemed to have impact and I use to love to leave a lasting impression. I didn't care if it made me look bad as a person, because everybody I hung around cursed too. So who was going to correct me? I just wanted to be the best curser of the group. I remember I used to look at myself in the mirror and make faces and point my finger and twirl my neck as I practiced all the things I was going to say to whoever ended up on my bad side that day.

I took so much pride in cursing I had imaginary trophies that I awarded myself after giving someone a good tongue-lashing. It was all about the win. I was good at having great and fast comebacks in arguments too. It was as if my brain had been storing up information on everyone I knew that had done something that maybe I didn't like or was just subconsciously waiting on them to trip with me so I could go off.

My first husband used to get it. I would curse him out so badly that when I finished tearing him down he would be in silence and I would be out of breath. I would be standing back looking at him as if I was daring him to say a word, just any word, a mutter, a stutter, anything because if he did, I had some more from where that came from. I was proud of my skill.

Oh yes it takes skills to be able to curse like that. Plus you had to be able to think fast on your feet to have a comeback if your opponent was good as well. You had to know when to go for the jugular.

I remember times when my friends would call me to tell me about an argument they had with someone. I would be listening to what the person said, then to what they said. I would get so mad because I would feel like they didn't say enough to win the argument. I would say, girl you should've told that Bleep, bleep, bleep, bleep, bleep, bleep and bleep. Then I would say, let's call her or him back and I'll talk. I wanted to get in on that action because nobody could serve it up like me. One friend would say, "Girl how do you think of all that to say so fast?" I would smile to myself thinking that's because I practice. Of course I never told her that, lol.

How I Tamed My Tongue

So how does a person who was a Certified Curser tame their tongue? As I said before when I made the decision to give my life to Christ that meant everything, my whole being. I wanted everything that God had for me, which meant I had to be serious about my walk. I asked the Lord to help me to tame my tongue. *I prayed, Lord please help me to use a better choice of words. Help me to hear myself so loud that the words would amplify in my own ear. If you see fit Lord, you can even allow me to bite my tongue, well Lord not literally, please don't let my tongue bleed, and just a small sting would do. Lord let me see your face every time I think about cursing.* I was pleading and negotiating asking the Lord to cleanse my potty mouth.

Slowly my words begin to change. I began to hear myself and I didn't like what I heard. I started hearing others around me cursing and I didn't like the sound anymore. I use to have the nerve to try to correct them. Shame on me; Ms. Curser herself! I think we all have come to a point in our lives where we no longer do something so we think automatically the people around us should stop too. No, sorry, it doesn't work like that. We have to remember that we all started somewhere at different times of our journey and we don't all move at the same pace. I'm not going to tell you that I never curse now but I will tell you that I am not the Champion anymore. I no longer win trophies and I am no longer proud of speaking with a corrupt tongue. I am still a work in progress but I do try to be more aware of my communication. If you have this issue, I would recommend you first have the desire to change how you communicate, even when under fire. Then pray and ask God to deliver you from corrupt communication, if you mean it, he will do just that.

You know what's so crazy right now? My current husband is a "Curser". Oh yes this brother has me beat even from back in the day on my best days. He curses so much that when I first starting dating him, I was like I think this might be a deal breaker. I listened to him communicate with his family and quickly realized that he came from a family of cursers. He inherited the cursing gene. I said God has a sense of humor! Remember in the above paragraph I said just because you stop doing something you can't expect everyone else to stop doing it too. God turned the mirror back on me. He showed me that just like he delivered me, he could deliver my husband.

One day I decided to ask him if he ever thought about not cursing. You may not believe me, but I promise this is the truth, his exact words were, "No, I haven't thought about quitting because I love how the words sound." He said I can stop if I want to, but I don't want to. As much as I didn't want to hear that, God showed me myself again and where he had brought me from. So now, I just pray for my husband and allow him to communicate however he feels he needs to get his words across because I know that day will come when it will also be his testimony too.

Ephesians 4:29 "*Let no corrupt communication proceed out of your mouth, but that which is good to the use of edifying, that he may minister grace unto the hearers.*"

It is written: (KJV) Proverbs 10:19 "*In the multitude of words there wanteth not sin: but he that refraineth his lips is wise.*"

CHAPTER FOUR

Lesson 4: Everything Is Not For Social Media

Everything is not for social media! Let's repeat, "Everything is not for social media."

Everyone who hits like isn't cheering with you and everyone who comments agreeing with you doesn't have your best interest at heart. There should be a "*shut-up grace button*" so we can help keep each other be more accountable.

Use social media wisely. There was a time when I didn't use it so wisely and it taught me the valuable lesson that "Everything isn't for social media." I had to practice by typing what I wanted to say, then reading it out loud to myself, and then deleting it. It was my form of release. I felt like I posted it and I guess it was an inner vent between cyber world, God, and me. I was always proud of myself for deleting childish or irresponsible things that I would've surely regretted later. Once you click post it's gone and there's no turning back. You can delete it after you post it but I guarantee someone has already taken a screenshot of your posted drama. People love drama, pay attention to how many more likes and shares you get for a positive stat versus a negative one. My husband always says, "*If you set yourself on fire people will come to watch you burn.*" This is a very true saying! Now after many lessons learned or after reading other stats on my timeline, I try to only post or share happy times, encouraging posts, videos, Fashion Remix Boutique business, prayers, and scriptures. If someone were to read my timeline I want them to say she is a positive God-fearing woman who cares about her business, her family, and her health. She loves her husband, her children, grandchildren, and her friends, end of story. If my husband and I are having issues, it won't be posted as a stat on social media. Some things need to stay between you, the person, and God.

Testimony

I have hid people from my timeline that constantly post negative stats or inappropriate crap that I care not to see. I have been deleted by former friends and once even by a family member who felt I was posting about her. Funny thing about that is I wasn't posting about her; as a matter of fact I hadn't even spoken with her for several weeks and I didn't notice that she had deleted me for about a month. When I finally realized it, I called her to ask if she deleted me because I was actually shocked. She said yes because you posted something that I thought was about me and also I noticed that you had not been clicking like on any of my stats lately. On the inside I laughed!

I didn't laugh out loud because I didn't want her to know how childish I thought she sounded. I simply took a deep breath and explained to her that none of my stats were about her. In fact there were other things going on in my life at the time that the stat or shared post related to. I wasn't posting to be mean to anyone but actually hoping the message would resonate with someone it may have applied to. I did a timeline evaluation and went scrolling back for one year; I didn't find anything negative directed towards anyone. As for me not clicking like on her stats, I explained that I wasn't on Facebook that often throughout the past couple of weeks and I either didn't see her stats or saw it but didn't agree and therefore, I didn't click like. Isn't that what the like button is for? You have the option to comment or click like if you actually like what was posted. Maybe I was tripping.

My point is that social media shouldn't become a source of validation for anyone. The number of likes you get shouldn't validate your message. Whomever your stat was meant to reach, it will reach and glory to God for that. Everything isn't for everyone to like and that should be okay. It was this encounter and others that made me more mindful about what I post and what I share. It's really not that serious anyway or is it?

This was a misunderstanding that could've gone left if I had not handled the conversation the way I did. My flesh wanted to burst out laughing and then say exactly how I felt but the God in me said for me to shut-up.

Think about the times when you're going through something that you know that only God can help you out of. Whatever time came to your mind just now, keep in mind how you feel and note that when you feel this way, it isn't the time to post a stat on social media. It's not the time to have a pity party, it isn't the time to get a glass of wine, nor to smoke a blunt! Instead, it is time to be 100% with yourself and accept that if God don't help you, then you can't be helped. This is also the time to activate "Shut-up grace." I recommend fasting and praying until you hear from God.

Remember people love drama. If you ever want to test the theory, make up a negative stat or video some kind of drama concerning your relationship and watch the likes stack up. Don't be surprised if it goes viral.

So many times we want to share what's going on in our lives with others. There's nothing wrong with that as long as you share with those people who are rowing in your boat not poking holes waiting to watch you sink.

Work Sheet:

1. What story does your social media timeline say about you? Do you need a Shut-up Grace Banner as your cover photo?

2. I challenge you to go to your social media page and review back at least one year of what type of stats you post. Write down 3 words to describe the type of stats you post.

1.

2.

3.

3. If your previous stats were not positive, ask yourself how can you clean up your timeline to present an impression that would be pleasing to the Lord?

4. I challenge you to ask someone that you trust and care about to do an evaluation of your social media timeline (Facebook, Instagram, Twiter, etc.). Write down the words that they used to describe your timeline in their honest opinion.

Write those words below:

____

____

I challenge you to pray daily and ask God for the spirit of conviction and discernment every time you get into your flesh and want to post something negative or distasteful or unpleasing to God on your social media pages. (This includes pictures)

CHAPTER FIVE

Lesson 5: How To Deal With Family & Friends

"Asking and Seeking Godly Wisdom"

The topic of shut-up grace falling on the same subject line as family and friends lets you know right away that there's going to be some hurt feelings and possibly broken relationships. Let's talk about ways to use wisdom when having to exercise this great art when communicating with those very close to us. There have been many occasions that I have spoken about a sensitive subject without thinking about the feelings of the person I was speaking with. When you are on the receiving end of information that you may not be ready to hear, it isn't a good feeling. I don't hold myself as the Judge nor the jury however, I will offer my honest advice when asked and sometimes even if not asked. I have learned many hard lessons and revelations in my life and most of which were very large pills to swallow and frankly, I already have a hard time swallowing small pills.

As a mother raising 3 very hardheaded sons, I would often try to pacify, support to no end, and even make excuses for their bad choices. I believe in them so much that often times I didn't realize that I was enabling them based on their potential. We want to see the best in our children even when they continue to show us the total opposite. My faith tells me that my sons are great men of God and integrity. This is me speaking life beyond what I see in the natural state. In reality with the natural eye, they continue to show me something very different. When I came to the realization that I can't pray my sons into change, or into the men that I know that God destined them to be, a huge load was lifted. This weight lifted didn't signify me giving up on my sons because that would mean I have given up on God. This merely means that I have come to a place of accepting God's will and the journey that they have chosen to travel until their change comes. God gives us free will and therefore it is by our own choices that we reroute God's plan for our lives. As an experienced parent, God allows me to see what my sons don't see on the way ahead. I can see how rocky the road is and that a train is coming fast but it's not up to me to decide when they should make a U-turn. As a caring and praying mother, this is hard to accept but since I truly have faith in God, I will trust him at all times.

I have the challenge of recognizing when I need to allow those close to me to vent and when I should offer advice. I told you, back in my introduction, that I'm not a bandwagon friend. Well, now I'm telling you that I'm not a bandwagon family member either. This rule of mine goes for anyone! Family or friend, I will not jump on your bandwagon when I feel that you're wrong but it's "Shut-up grace" that tells me to be quiet and pray. It has also helped me to see that God is in control and my situation with my sons may not be the same journey that another may be having, although their situation resembles mine. I have to pray and trust God for them and their children, the same way I pray and believe God for my children. Because of shut-up grace, I have learned to always trust and believe him for my friends and family.

For instance, there have been many situations where someone close to me was dating someone that I felt was all-wrong for them. All the warning signs were flashing and I believe they knew the person was wrong for them as well. Sometimes we choose to walk through matters of the heart very blindly and I can recognize it because I too know that experience very well. We make a choice to ignore God or we fool ourselves into believing that God has blessed the relationship and therefore, we will stick it out until disaster strikes. The problem lies when we don't learn from our mistakes and continue to make the same type of mistakes year after year, from one person to the next. I believe when I see someone I care about making the same mistakes over and over, I have an obligation to say something and of course, this has gotten me in trouble a few times. Why? Possibly the receiver wasn't ready to receive what I had to say. Possibly, it came out as harsh or insensitive. Possibly, and very likely, the truth hurts.

If I pray over a situation that I am led to say something about, I believe that I delivered it the way it was meant to be delivered. Otherwise, I will never say anything. Regardless of my delivery, I have lost friends and have experienced major family feuds. You may ask how God is in that if you end things on a bad note. My answer is that some things and some people are only in your life for a season. It is inevitable that some things and some people have an expiration date in your life. In many cases, you pray that your loved ones will eventually get over the issue and you will be able to move on in love.

In every situation that has ended on a bad note, I sought the wisdom of God first. I trusted him during the process and I trusted him with the results. It was because of this, I was able to have a great sense of peace and love for the other person even though they were very angry with me. I only hope that if I am in a state of mess; someone will care enough about me to seek Godly wisdom and share with me whatever needs to be said, no matter how hurtful the issue is. I also pray that I am able to take it like a woman and receive it in love.

Testimony

If you're married and you have a mother-in-law or in-laws that poses challenges to your marriage you will want to pay close attention to what you're about to read. If you're single and desire to get married or have a significant other who you plan to marry in the future you should pay attention as well. I want to bless you but just know you may need to read this more than once to really get this in your spirit. If you have a mother-in-law or family members that you have a great relationship with, you should thank God everyday!

This is my story and I'll tell you upfront that this isn't about my current mother-in-law. Nevertheless, in the past, I had a mother-in-law from hell. I heard all the stories about when you marry someone you marry their family however I never believed that. I lived in a world where I only married the man who stood next to me in front of God and others to say, "I Do". Let's just say I am now a believer that you truly marry the family as well. I was once lost but now I'm found!

My husband, at that time, struggled with spoiling me without feeling like he had to spoil his mother. If he bought things for me, he had to buy for his mom. It was not only an intense struggle for him but also a severe issue for his mother. If he bought anything for our home, it was like his momma had a radar and antenna because she always seemed to make a visit at the very time he added things to our home. She seemed to notice anything new and then would ask her son to purchase the same thing or something very similar. He didn't know how to say no and if I said something about it to him, I became the bad guy. I couldn't like his momma because if he didn't have an issue with it, then why should I? My thought was that we're married, we have children, we have a house, we have bills, why are you trying to take care of our household and your momma's? To top it off she was married herself!

I never had a problem with his dad but I'm guessing I wouldn't since it's just something about two women who love the same man. When two women love the same man, you're going to have issues every time. We would argue about his mom and her projecting herself into our business all the time. We would argue about him spending money to please her even it was stretching our budget. There was even a time when I decided to take matters into my own hands and say something to her myself. This put an instant wedge between she and I. She felt like I was trying to steal her son and in turn, began to say things about me to him, which caused lots of problems in our marriage. I was at the end of my rope. How do you compete with a man's momma? Furthermore, this shouldn't be a competition.

I found out that my answer is, you don't. It was a hard lesson to learn but let me tell you that once I learned the secret, I was at peace and my marriage began to heal in that area. Honestly, it really isn't a secret but more like a revelation of wisdom.

Whenever you have the battle of the sexes when it involves matters of the heart remember these things:

1. Pray without ceasing

2. Know your lane, stay in it, and don't veer to the left or to the right.

3. Become the peacemaker! This means that anytime you can humble yourself to bring peace, you will get an optimal outcome. God sees it and your husband will soon notice too.

4. Never speak ill about your partner's mother to him. If you need to vent, tell God or someone you trust that will not be on your band-wagon. You need someone who will be truthful with you or who will offer wisdom from a spiritual perspective.

5. The more you practice being nice to your mother-in-law or in-laws who continue to be vindictive towards you, eventually their characteristics

and behaviors will be exposed. Your partner will see exactly what they're doing. This may not happen overnight and it will be important to have patience, pray without ceasing, and trust God. You may even have to separate yourself although not to the point where you become non-existent. Continue to attend gatherings for the sake of your husband. He will love you for this. Find a mutual person in the family to spend time around when the unpleasant ones or present. Be respectful, don't be a doormat, and always remember it isn't about them anyway. God will fix it and he doesn't need your help.

The more I did these things, the more my mother-in-law showed her claws. Eventually something wonderful happened. My husband started venting to me about things his mother was doing and saying that seemed to make him upset. He began to say all the things that I had been saying about her all along. I would sit quietly while smiling and sometimes even laughing on the inside. Everything in me wanted to say, "I told you so! Yes! You finally see this evil witch for the person she is".

You know I didn't say it but I was thinking it! The more she pushed with her tactics, the more he started staying away from her. He went from stopping by her house every day to missing several months. She would tell people, "Oh my son is mad at me". She started calling wanting to talk to me saying how she missed the kids and she hadn't seen us in a while but needless to say, it wasn't long enough for me. I was so thankful to the Lord for exposing her. He finally felt what I felt. She didn't like being isolated so when we began to come around her again, there was a major change in her attitude. I also believe she began to trust me and realized that her son was happy in his marriage. She saw that she could still play an important role in her son's life and that I was not a threat. We shared important but different roles in his life and there was room for the both of us.

I urge you that if you have ever or if you're struggling with a situation that involves a man's mother, children, or siblings, please pray and follow the tips I provided. In every situation, if you learn to put God in the center and do the right thing, I guarantee you will have a much better outcome.

Example: The Powers of Words

I once had a friend who was going through a difficult time in her marriage. She thought her mother-in-law didn't like her. I just so happened to know her mother-in-law and spoke with her on different occasions. I knew first-hand what her mother-in-law thought about her. She actually loved her and thought she was great for her son. Unfortunately, no matter how much I tried to convince her that she was all wrong, she never could seem to wrap her mind around the concept to believe me. I would offer advice and wisdom on Godly ways to continue to show love and share with her the ways that she could do her part and how God would bless her marriage simply because of her obedience to please God and her husband.

The poor husband was torn between the two women; wife and momma. They would argue about his mother and eventually other family members too. He started attending family functions without his wife because she didn't want to be in the same room with those that she felt didn't care for her. I offered advice about this. I told my friend that she should go for her husband. I said be nice, speak, and be respectful; but cling to your husband if you're feeling uncomfortable. I believe she tried this once or twice, but just couldn't bring herself to a place of submission or humility. I told her, "Girl! Your husband will love you that much more if you're there for his sake."

Well, to make a long story short, they started having other issues that were only escalating. It got so bad that my friend started saying things like, "I'm leaving him" and "He doesn't deserve me anyway". One day she said it to a group of our girlfriends. Some laughed with her and some didn't think it was cute or funny. I pulled her to the side and to let her know that she was wrong and that speaking negative about your husband in public and not wearing your ring is setting your marriage up for destruction. She said she wasn't trying to hear me and so, I left her alone.

One day, in the middle of the morning, she called me. She was crying so hard, I could barely understand what she was saying. I was so startled that I rushed up out of my bed to get my bearings and to go to another room to talk. I didn't want to wake my husband and I was not sure if I was about to be crying with her, screaming, praying or what. I just knew that my friend was calling me at 2:00 am so something had to be terribly wrong. When she finally calmed down enough to the point that I could understand what she was trying to say, I heard the words loud and clear, "My husband is leaving me." "He's packing right now."

Instantly, I thought back to that day that she said she was leaving him. I started having flashbacks to all those times that I labored with her in prayer, long talks, and just offering encouragement regarding her marriage. I thought about all those times that I said you better watch what you put into the atmosphere. I held the phone speechless as all those memories begin to flood my mind.

She finally stopped long enough to say "*Tonita, are you there?*" I blatantly said, "Yes. I'm just trying to understand why you're so upset. You have been saying this for over a year now. I would've thought you would be relieved right now. Are you upset because he beat you to the punch?" She began to say how she had changed her mind and how she decided she really wanted to be with her husband. She never wanted a divorce and she wanted to work things out. Unfortunately, her husband didn't feel the same way.

Now of course this isn't the only thing that happened to bring them to their final destination in their marriage however I learned another valuable lesson about how powerful our words can be. You have to watch what you say because the same words you put out can have a way of manifesting in a way that you're not prepared to deal with.

Worksheet:

Ask yourself do you have a special prayer for a family member or friend?

Is there something that you want to seek God about concerning a loved one and you're not sure if you should say anything?

Is there a pressing issue that deserves God's attention? If so, what is it?

Do you recognize a situation that could have detrimental effects if you don't say anything?

Do you exercise the power of shut-up grace with friends and family?

What hard lessons have you learned?

What can you do different to gain God's favor?

CHAPTER SIX

Lesson 6: They Have Weeds, Just Like You

"Stop looking at someone else's life"

Let's just get this out of the way at the very beginning of this chapter, just because what another couple shows you from the outside looking inside, doesn't mean every day is a sun shiny day in their world. Nobody is going to give you a front row ticket to their mess! People show you what they want to show you. Do you really think they're going to share the details of their messed up relationship with you? They will allow you to see a pretty picture of their garden, but what you don't see are the weeds they've hidden underneath the flowers. If your relationship, marriage, or whatever arrangement you're involved in has begun to grow weeds then I urge you to pull the weeds and begin to water your own garden daily. In other words, focus on what God has blessed you with, pray for things to get better, and do your part by working on things daily. Pray without ceasing!

Now, if you are married or plan to get married one day, please let me be a blessing to you. Repeat these words: "**Everything and every situation will not need a response**." Repeat that 3 times or as many times as you need to, to get it in your spirit. This is very hard for a lot of women and yes, I said women. I am raising my hand too so don't think I'm picking on the ladies. If we are honest we must admit ladies we have a spirit that dwells in us that just has to have the last word. Why is this? The bible tells us in Proverbs 14:1, *A wise woman builds her house while the foolish woman tears hers down with her own hands.* My God, that's powerful. We all need to meditate on that scripture daily, wives, soon to be wives, and want to be wives.

How terrible would it be to be labeled as the foolish woman who tore down her own house with her hands? Many marriages have ended from a foolish woman who tore down her husband, her children, and then single-handedly tore down her whole house. Ladies we have to stay on our face and our knees before God and ask for wisdom daily to discern how to communicate first with God and then with our husbands. Do you know that if you seek God in all things he will deal with any issue you have about your husband. Just remember; he will first show you yourself.

It is written: (KJV) Proverbs 3:5-6 "*Trust in the LORD with all thine heart; and do not lean unto thine own understanding. In all thy ways acknowledge him, and He shall direct thy paths.*"

We all have something about our husbands that we want God to fix when the fact of the matter is, we need to pray and ask God to fix us. If we focus on pleasing God and getting ourselves together, God will do the work in our husbands. If you're not married but you desire to be married, you should be praying and asking God to prepare you to be the wife/husband that God wants you to be for your mate that is prepared for you. God won't prepare you to be the spouse for someone else's spouse. Remember that!

My husband isn't the quiet type. He is a jack of all trades. He's a go-getter that's about his money and his business. He decided to stop working for other people years ago to become a full-time entrepreneur. He has been a part of many business ventures and is now running his own Real Estate Company called Smith's Homes. Don't get me wrong he's not all business; he can also be the life of the party and a big talker at times and more so a jokester which is probably a better way to describe him. He's very handsome and charming and most people tend to be drawn to him, especially women. Over the years of getting to know him, his personality, and character, I've learned several valuable lessons. The first thing is when he loves, he loves hard and he's very loyal. With loyalty comes trust and there has to be a solid foundation in which he feels comfortable and safe to allow all walls to come down. I knew very quickly I had to be very confident and trustworthy to be allowed into the deepest part of his make-up. As women, some may think as long as you please your man sexually and clean the house and do what's expected then you're good to go. I'm here to tell you that all those things are much needed however, if you ever want to connect on a deeper level and actually become best friends with your mate, you have to get to know him and allow him to know you on every level.

We've all heard the cliché' "*Soul mate*" but what does it really mean to be someone's soul mate? Does it mean simply to be compatible, attracted to, or liking all of the same things? Can you truly be yourself with that person, do you have effective communication with one another even when there's nobody else around, and can you spend hours together just enjoying each other's company doing absolutely nothing? Can you pray together, play together, cook together, clean together, and build together? Do you anticipate seeing them at the end of your day? Do you know when it's time for silence? Can you anticipate their needs, thoughts, or even finish their sentence? I know this all sounds like a fairy tale, and we all know there is no perfect relationship, but I'm here to tell you that it can come very close. When you connect with the person God intended for you to be with as life partners, you will make harmonious music! You will build, complement, and balance each other very well. This is all built upon a solid foundation from the very beginning.

Having prior marriages and then divorces, I never thought this kind of love existed. I also knew I wasn't the type of woman who could date the same man for more than 2 years without committing to a future or calling the quits. I've never pressured nor asked a man to marry me. I believe it is something about how a woman carries herself that tells the right man that she is meant to be a wife; not a girlfriend forever. As women we set the standard for how we desire to be treated. I joke around all the time when people compliment my relationship with my husband by saying, "*Yes, I kissed 2 frogs before I kissed my prince.*" I could've given up and threw in the towel. I could've done a lot of other things like decided to be alone and bitter, but God said no. I told God that I was content with being single and loving him. I told God I guess I don't need a mate because I keep striking out. God allowed me to get in a quiet space and he healed my broken heart and disappointment.

I found a renewed reassurance in the fact that I made some mistakes, but I wasn't going to allow my mistakes to become my destiny. I knew who I was and I knew I had so much love to share with a deserving person. I knew that God had prepared me to be a great wife to my partner; unfortunately I allowed the wrong men to enter into my life and that wasn't God's plan for me. Let's just say I had to learn the hard way but thankfully, my past led me to a much better future.

I exercised shut-up grace and allowed God to take control. Whatever was going to be was going to be. I just wanted to walk in my purpose. I began to bury myself in the things of God. I started exercising more, spending more time with my grandson, and overall enjoying my life. I wasn't going to be some bitter woman who was mad at men and at the world because my plans didn't work out as I hoped for. I was going to take responsibility for my shortcomings, learn from my mistakes, and move forward in peace and happiness.

Just as I was entering my last year in nursing school, a man came into my life and literally swept me off my feet. I was drawn to him by his blunt, confident, bold, and honest spirit. They say if you ever meet a true Sagittarius man you will understand what I'm talking about. In the beginning, I didn't really know how to take him because he was very different from any man I had ever dated before. He had goals, he was motivated, driven, knew exactly what he wanted, and he knew exactly how to go for it and make it happen. He courted me; we went on dates almost every day. He was very creative, and thoughtful with each date, this intrigued me even more. Of course I played hard to get initially because again, I was not used to someone so confident and so aggressive with a take-charge type of attitude. Quite often I prayed, "*Lord please show me what the intent of this man's heart is.*" I gave him a 10-question quiz that I had received from a women's ministry. He passed with an 80%. I thought to myself, well Lord I'm not 100% so how can I expect this man to be 100% perfect; I'll take an 80/20. I pride myself in never being any man's booty call and I didn't get to this age to become one now. So I prayed again, "Lord if he is not for me, remove him now, show me a sign and I will run like Forrest Gump." I went on a 7 day fast and I prayed to God with everything in me. When I fast, meaning I give up something that isn't very easy to do, I can hear God the loudest. Fasting combined with prayer allows intimate time to fellowship with the Father. Through fasting, I am saying to the Lord, I need you, I need to hear you, no distractions, just me and you Lord. I just didn't want to be distracted or to be led by my flesh in any way. I was getting too old to keep making the same mistakes with my choosing of men for the wrong reasons.

While I was fasting and praying, God was dealing with the man I was dating. He came to me just 2 weeks into our courtship and said "I love you.' I was caught off guard but honestly I felt the same way. Next, he said, "You're going to be my wife". I was thinking God hasn't told me that but surprisingly, God revealed it to me 3 days later with the instruction, "Stop trying to fight this. He is your husband".

The rest is history in the making. We have our ups and downs like any married couple, but I can honestly say it's been far more ups then downs and I am thankful for that. In every trial, we've come out stronger as we continue to work through any issues the enemy throws our way.

It isn't that trouble won't come; it's just that when you're connected with the right person, you're able to climb the mountain together. The key is putting God in everything, trusting God, and working together to master coping skills through prayer and supplication, which will get you through anything. When you put God first and your faith is so strong, no matter what the devil tries to through your way, you will still get through it because you have chosen to trust God no matter what.

When you connect with whom God has placed in your life, their presence will make you better. Your significant other should add to you and vice versa. You are to be each other's biggest supporter and are to always uplift each other, especially behind closed doors and then in the presence of others. My husband can say he wants to sell ice-cream, I will be right by his side scooping. That's how tight your bond should be with your mate. If it's not illegal, or immoral, you should support each other, end of story.

I pray that every woman or man, married or single reading this book will be blessed to connect with the companion that God intends for your life. I recommend every married person to pray and seek God daily concerning your marriage and your spouse. Every single person should pray and ask God to begin to prepare them for the mate that God has for them. You want to be prepared when God sends your helpmate. There is nothing worse than being unprepared for such a significant moment destined by God.

Let's visit a few couples with hidden weeds: James and Victoria have been married for 20 years and have no children. They are both college graduates and have great professional careers making a combined income of over $200,000 per year. They live in the suburbs, both drive luxury cars, dress very fashionably, and attend church occasionally. James is what many women would refer to as a "*great catch*". Victoria, on the other hand, is considered "*average looking*" but very confident. Victoria is also a social butterfly and has lots of followers on all her social media platforms. She loves to post pictures of herself, her material items, her home, cars, vacations, family, etc. James is a little more low-key when it comes to social media however, he does frequent the sites. From the outside or from Victoria's social media platforms, her marriage to James looks like the perfect marriage made in heaven. Many followers comment on her pictures referring to them as a power couple. Many envy their marriage based on what they are allowed to see.

What people don't know is that, James has cheated on Victoria with 4 different women at different stages of their marriage. Just last year Victoria was threatening to divorce him for the 3rd time. Victoria is somewhat afraid to divorce him even though the trust has been completely broken.

The last time Victoria saw an attorney regarding a divorce, the attorney advised her that because of the assets they share, she would be best served if they were to stay together.

Victoria doesn't have anyone that she feels she can trust to share how unhappy she really is in her marriage. Victoria is also a perfectionist who doesn't want to feel like a failure and therefore it is the combination of all these things that have kept her in her unhappy marriage.

Victoria used to dread going home but now she's gotten so good at pretending that everything is okay and therefore this life has become normal for her. She knows just how to smile for the cameras and pose in strategic positions that camouflage her true body language of not wanting James to touch her.

James and Victoria both realize that they have a dysfunctional marriage however; neither wants to be the one to end it for their own selfish reasons. They will probably stay in their marriage until something gives.

In this example, if James and Victoria really wanted to rekindle the love that brought them together in the first place, somebody in this marriage is going to have to get saved. If at least one partner is standing in the gap for the other one and activating prayer and faith for their marriage to be restored, God can deliver the other spouse and restore their marriage stronger than ever before.

This is why we can't allow ourselves to get caught up in what someone else's life looks like from the outside. Everything that sparkles is not gold or platinum. There are lots of counterfeits, knock-offs, and fakes out there. If you have been blessed with a spouse, learn to pray for your spouse and your marriage. This should be daily; like brushing your teeth. Covering your spouse in prayer should become your normal routine.

Did you know that the devil will use children, friends, family members, or anyone close to you to steal, kill, and destroy everything that you've worked hard for? If you leave a window open in your home or your door cracked and a robber is passing by, he is going to come inside. The devil is just like that robber, looking for broken marital foundations to slip inside and before you know it he has a room in your house. Before you know it he has moved in, gotten comfortable, and has moved you out of your own house.

I have a friend that we'll call Toya. She is married and has children. Toya is a God-fearing woman who has had her share of trials and tribulations. At this point in her life she truly deserves to be happy because I feel like she has sacrificed so much of herself for others. Don't get me wrong; Toya hasn't always been the nice Christian that I'm painting her out to be. She was once a fire-spitting rebel on my team as well. She was a fighter too! She would fight your momma, the kids, and anybody else if they wanted a piece.

Toya is someone who came from the hood but struggled to get out and actually made it out. She is a hard worker and has no intentions of ever going back to that life and would probably work 3 jobs, if she had to, just to make sure that never happened. From the outside looking in she appears to have a healthy and happy marriage.

The issue with Toya is somehow she has lost her way. She's married and has had to deal with some deal breaking moments that have broken her spirit in many ways. She loves her husband and wants to have peace in her home. I believe her husband loves her as well, but lacks the ability to love her in the way that she needs him too. She knows how to pray and I believe she prays for her marriage but whether she believes that God can and will fix it is the question.

Toya's husband struggles with alcohol abuse. He is a different person when he drinks and this person is someone she doesn't like to be around. The problem that I've noticed is that she wants him to give up the addiction but will drink with him from time to time. She hasn't really figured out how to deal with the problem but knows she can't make him stop drinking if it's not his choice. So since she can't make him stop, she has chosen to join him, which only makes things worse. Toya must learn to trust God at all times. She has to ask God to fix her so that he can be glorified through her example.

Toya will have to pray and ask God to help her to edify her husband and pray for him daily. She has to believe and have faith that God will deliver him.

I urge you to do a self-evaluation of everything the devil has stolen from you that you want back. Fast, pray, and walk boldly into his camp to take back everything the devil has stolen from you. Declare that the Lord has already given you the victory and the devil cannot have your stuff. Serve the devil his eviction notice and do a spiritual cleanse throughout your home, car, or whatever you feel represents the battlefield.

Worksheet:

If you were to do a self-evaluation, what things would you want the Lord to help you to change?

Do you know of another couple that you have tried to pattern your relationship after? If so, write their names.

I challenge you to write a prayer asking the Lord to help you to pull the weeds out of your own garden. Ask for release of this other couple from your thoughts. Ask the Lord to help you to find your way back to your own partner.

CHAPTER SEVEN

Lesson 7: Never Say Never

"How to handle workplace blues"

Let's face it! We've all had the one co-worker or boss that absolutely knew how to get under our skin. It could've been the sound of their annoying voice, or the way they came across in meetings, or just simply the way they looked at you. Regardless of what the real issue was, they always seemed to rub you the wrong way.

I'd like to share a personal experience with you about how I was tested to deal with someone on my job that seemed to rub me the wrong way. I hope it blesses you and if you're ever put into a similar situation, I want you to remember my story and how God allowed me to be tested so that he could deliver me.

Let's call the lady Ms. Jessie. I was a nurse supervisor at a small pediatric clinic and Ms. Jessie was the receptionist. Ms. Jessie was a strange looking lady and she wore this up-do style ponytail that was braided to the middle of her back and not a hair out of place either. Did I mention this was a weave ponytail? Nevertheless, Ms. Jessie had a walk that turned heads and I don't mean in a good way. She wore a frown on her face that said "I'm not approachable so please don't speak or talk to me." She had a masculine toned voice and very hard features. I think you get the picture. She was not an attractive woman to say the least.

Ms. Jessie always arrived to work on time. I later learned that she would leave home early enough to catch the bus, which allowed her plenty of time to get to work and eat a little something before our doors opened for the morning. Keep in mind that this is a pediatric clinic so you can imagine we had lots of noisy crying babies and toddlers running around. Our lobby area usually resembled a playground. One day I got the bright idea to purchase some movies to bring in for the children to watch in the waiting area in hopes of getting their attention to possibly settle them down. This seemed to work on most days. I would come in to work, speak to Ms. Jessie who never spoke back and then my Medical Assistant and Pediatrician. I loved this job! We were all like a little family, all except Ms. Jessie. She never seemed happy about anything. The Medical Assistant and I were always having a good time with the children and making jokes throughout the day to pass the time. Ms. Jessie on the other hand thought we were silly little girls who played too much and she wanted no part of our fun.

One day when the office was empty of patients, the medical assistant and I decided to try to hold a conversation with her. We asked questions like do you have any kids? What do you like to do for fun? Every question we asked she had a yes or no answer with any real feedback. This told me that she was not interested in sharing who she really was to either of us.

Over the next few weeks we went back to ignoring Ms. Jessie and just talking amongst each other while doing our job. Ms. Jessie strated being extremely rude to me. She started by calling me by my last name instead of my first name. At that time my last name was "Williams." She would call out to me in a very abrasive tone, "Williams, you need to get this paper." Or "Williams" somebody is here to see you. She would make other rude remarks. Once a male friend called me on the phone and she yelled out in the clinic; "Williams, some man is on the phone for you, but ain't you married?" I tried my best to ignore her because our waiting room was full. As I went to answer the phone I could see all the parents staring at me as if they wanted to know who was on the phone as well. I took the call then quickly hung up the phone. I could feel Ms. Jessie glaring at me as I walked away too mad to say a word. She chuckled as to say, I know I got under your skin.

I waited until the clinic closed for the day and then I went to her and said, "Can I talk to you?" She said, "No" and got up from her chair, picked up her purse and walked out the door. I believe I failed to mention that I was Ms. Jessie's immediate Supervisor although I had nothing to do with the hiring process. I would have to write her up and pass it along to my boss, which was the big boss.

The next day when I came to work and as usual I spoke to her, she stared at me, and never said a word. I walked into my office and took a deep breath. I walked back out to the reception desk after about 5 minutes before any patients were there. I said, "Did I do something to offend you Ms. Jessie?" She looked me straight in the eyes and said, "No, I just don't like you."

"You don't have to like me, but you do have to work with me and you do have to respect me," I responded. I wanted to say so much more but the Holy Ghost inside of me was keeping my flesh under arrest. She looked at me with the same stare and said, "No I don't."

I said, "Ms. Jessie you do realize that I am your supervisor?."

I politely told her, "I have the authority to write you up and recommend you for termination due to insubordination." She retorted with, "I don't have to like you; as long as I do my job."

I walked away because I had to go calm down. In my mind I was saying, "I should just curse her out, I've never had to deal with something or somebody that irks my soul like this before. I can quit this job! It would be easy for me to get another job then to deal with this."

Part of what she said was correct. She did do her job, even if it was mediocre. I had to go outside to get into my car to pray. I asked God to help me to hold my tongue. I wanted God to know that I was weak but I didn't want to take the easy way out by going off on this lady. I would then be just as bad as her if I fought fire with fire. I recognized the test but I felt that I was going to lose the battle if Ms. Jessie said one more disrespectful thing to me.

I came back inside with red eyes because when I go to God it's such a powerful connection when I feel his presence that I always get emotional. I tried not to look Ms. Jessie's way but I could feel her staring at me with a smirk on her face. I wanted to smack that smirk right off her face but the Holy Ghost in me wouldn't allow it. I kept saying to myself, Why Lord? Why me? And the Lord responded, "*Why not you?*"

I went back into my office and the Medical Assistant entered to see if I was okay. She told me that Ms. Jessie was talking crap about me when I left out. She was saying stuff like yeah, she thinks she's so perfect and so holy but we are going to see how saved she really is. It was at that moment that I knew that she was being used by the enemy to test my faith. I was going into spiritual warfare and there was no turning back. This enemy just showed his face and made his mission known.

The following weekend, I attended a woman's conference gathering at my church. The ladies were all sitting in a circle and took turns discussing things that were happening in their lives, which they need prayer for. When my turn came, I was a little hesitant to share my issues about Ms. Jessie because I felt like it was nothing compared to some of the other prayer requests that were going forth. I decided to share anyway because it was weighing very heavy on my heart. I had even contemplated quitting the job that I loved so much just to get away from her.

Why didn't I just write her up and recommend she be terminated? Although I knew I had that option, the Lord never led me in that direction. You see, even though Ms. Jessie had these ill feelings towards me I knew without a doubt that I had done nothing to deserve her disrespect. I also knew that she needed her job as evidenced by her catching the bus and walking 3 blocks to get to work so early in the morning. I knew that Ms. Jessie's issues would require God's love and deliverance and this was not my battle.

As I told the ladies about the situation, one of the elders began to pray for Ms. Jessie and I at the very moment. When she was done, I felt as if a load had been lifted off my shoulders. This was another very valuable lesson I learned that day. Never keep your mouth shut when the enemy is attacking you, speaking the situation was a way of exposing the enemy and all his tricks. The weapon was formed but it could not and would not prosper.

It is written: (KJV) Isaiah 54:17 "*No weapon that is formed against thee shall prosper; and every tongue that shall rise against thee in judgment thou shalt condemn. This is the heritage of the servants of the Lord, and their righteousness is of me, saith the Lord.*"

The elder told me to continue to go to work, smile, and speak everyday as I always had and don't even look for Ms. Jessie to speak back. She said to continue to be respectful and continue to enjoy my day regardless of what Ms. Jessie said and just show love. Lastly, she told me to start arriving to work earlier than Ms. Jessie. She gave me a bottle of blessed oil and told me to pray and apply bless oil in the area where she works. Don't say a word just pray for her, pray for peace in the workplace and put the cross sign in her chair, on the keyboard and computer, and in the cabinet where she places her purse.

Over the next week I did just that! I arrived bright and early before anyone else. I went into Ms. Jessie's reception area and prayed for her as if she was my sister and I put crosses everywhere that I thought she would touch or sit. I started going to my car everyday that week on my lunch break just to pray and have alone time with the Lord. This gave me a greater sense of peace to make it through the afternoons because it was something about that demonic spirit that really turned up after lunch. She continued to say little remarks towards me and to me and I continued to ignore her and show respect.

One day, the Medical Assistant told me that she didn't see how I allowed her to continue to talk crazy and disrespectful to me and how the patients are starting to talk about it in the lobby area. I told her, "Girl, God is working this thing out you just watch because you are going to be a witness." Two weeks later exactly on a Friday afternoon around 1:00 pm, Ms. Jessie returned from lunch and came and sat down and began to gather her things. She had a tote bag that she was putting her personal items into and she had her purse still on her shoulder. Without an uttered word she got up from her seat and began to walk out the door. The Medical Assistant called me to the window and said, "Look! Where is Ms. Jessie going? Did she quit?" I told her that the demonic spirit couldn't dwell in here any longer because the presence of God is here and it's too peaceful. Ms. Jessie never returned to work again and we never knew what happened to her or if she ever gave a reason as to why she quit her job.

What I did realize is that when God allows us to be tested it's so that we can have a testimony to help others and so that he may get the Glory. He will allow us to be put into uncomfortable situations because he is trying to take us to another level in him. I never forgot this lesson and the same principles have worked for me on other jobs since Ms. Jessie. Things may not have gone the same way but there were very similar situations where I had to realize the test and continue to show love by doing what's right and allowing God to fight the battle. Remember, workplace blues don't have to stay blue.

It is written: (KJV) Exodus 14:14,"*The LORD shall fight for you, and ye shall hold your peace.*"

Workbook: 1-2

1. Is there someone on your job that rubs you the wrong way or seems to poke you over and over again?

If so, how do you handle or communicate with that person?

2. Have you tried praying for them and the situation?

I challenge you to pray for them. I challenge you to give the situation to God and allow him to work it out. Write your prayer below.

Summary: Enough Said

Remember, you do not have to have the last word. Many times saying nothing at all is saying a mouthful. Pray and develop a close personal relationship with God. Develop a prayer life so strong that you will be able to feel his gentle nudge or his whisper that reminds you of your momma or daddy's look that meant, you better shut your mouth or else.

When we do things on our own based on moving in our flesh it is almost certain to go wrong but oh how sweet it is to move into God's timing and purpose. Things are always guaranteed to go right. God is so good that he makes no mistakes. He is a perfect God but we are not. Once you come to the realization of who you want to please more than yourself life will become more purpose driven.

Many times I made the mistake of looking at the situation because with my natural eye all I could see was destruction or pain. I wasn't looking with my spiritual eye so I would take matters into my own hands and try to fix or resolve the situation myself. In almost every case I caused more issues for myself making the issue bigger than it had to be. It was those times, when I learned to look with my spiritual eyes, that I saw God working it out. I was a recipient of the blessings for my obedience. God never gets it wrong! It may not come as fast as we want or it may not happen the way we imagined it but I'm a witness that he has always exceeded my expectations.

Praise Report

I can remember sharing my testimony with someone about buying a new car. It was never about the car for me because I was already driving a car that I was quite satisfied with. It was truly about the goodness of God and the favor he granted me in that specific situation. I was at the Plaza Motors dealership getting my Mercedes Benz 2013 C-300 serviced. It was just an oil change and whatever else comes with that. I was sitting in the customer lounge, as I always do, eating their free freshly popped popcorn and drinking water preparing to take a nap because they are so slow to me. On this day I was wide awake watching CNN News. I overheard one of the sales representatives say that the rapper Nelly was in the showroom. I have been to this dealership many times and I can count on one hand how many times I entered the showroom floor when I'm there to get my car serviced. I rarely go into the showroom because again, I was quite satisfied with the car I was driving.

I'm going to be very transparent! On this day, the only reason why I got up to enter the showroom floor was because I heard them say Nelly was in there. I know, call me vain a groupie or whatever but I went to be nosey and that's the truth. Just as I entered the showroom, Nelly was leaving out the door, so my nosey self only got to catch a glimpse of him. The receptionist must've saw my face because she immediately said, "Honey you just missed Nelly! He bought that beautiful car right there" as she pointed to a gorgeous black sporty Mercedes Benz. She went on to say he's coming back in 3 days to pick it up. Okay, I couldn't just go back to the lounge after that, so I played it off by walking around checking out their inventory on the floor. My eye was immediately drawn to a navy blue 2015 C-300 with a shiny brown wood polish dash interior. I walked over to admire the car a little bit closer and before I knew it I was opening the door sitting inside. I called my husband on the phone and was telling him the whole story about Nelly and the car he had purchased and how I was admiring this new updated version of my car. I said to myself, "Let's see.. I have 5 years left before I retire and if I am going to purchase a car that can be paid off by retirement, maybe the time is now. Then I wondered how much more would this car cost in comparison to my current comfortable car payment? If my payment could be $100 or less more per month I would buy this car today. Just as I said that a saleslady was very close by listening. She went and found out what car I had in the service department and began to crunch the numbers. She returned and said, I don't mean to listen to your conversation but I believe we can get you a great deal on this car today. It's the end of the month and we need to meet a quota. We can throw in lots of perks as well. I asked my husband to come to the dealership so that he could help me to make a wise decision, plus this was a major purchase and I honestly had no intentions of purchasing a new car. My husband showed up within 10-15 minutes and sure enough the lady came back and said, "We can get your payment at about $75 more and we will throw in a maintenance free package", which I didn't have with my current car. She also told me that they would add GAP insurance, which I had but I paid for it before, and they were willing to throw in an extended warranty, no money down, will pay off my trade completely, will cover the sales tax, and I'd get the car off the showroom floor that's fully loaded. Wow, I thought to myself this is too good to be true. My husband being the skeptic that he is, said put everything you just said in writing and we might have a deal. The lady went to speak with her sales manager and asked, "Can you guys stick around to sign the paperwork tonight? We are putting everything in writing and you can leave with the car tonight."

That deal was closed and this testimony is just a small fraction of what God has shown me about his plans, always exceeding my expectations.

I was not in the market to buy a new car but it took a situation, "Nelly being in the showroom", for God to get my attention, go into that same room, and to leave that night with a new blessing. It was all just because God did it and he said, "I want to bless you daughter."

We don't know why or how God does what he does. We just know that we want to be recipients of whatever he has for us. I am so thankful to God for everything that he has done and is doing in my life even though I don't feel deserving. I am humbly grateful.

I challenge you to develop a close relationship with the Father. Talk to him on a daily basis, throughout the day, or whenever you need guidance. God will not only hear your prayers but he will answer your prayers according to his will for your life.

Now we have come to a place where we are going to pray and ask God to fix us. My prayer for my life and anyone reading this is to ask God to, "*Show us ourselves. Help us Lord to walk in the purpose that you have for our lives. Help us to recognize when we need to put our flesh and our tongues under your submission. Help us in areas where we fall short. Decrease us so that you may be increased in us. Help us to do the things that will glorify you and bless others. Help us to be a blessing to others. Help us to use our words for the building of others and not for tearing others down.*"

Amen

About the Author

Author Tonita Smith is a married mother, grandmother, veteran, and RN residing in Missouri.

She loves helping others by promoting health wellness and prevention to many people from all cultures and backgrounds. She is a God-fearing Christian with the heart to serve others, especially Teens. She believes in the power of prayer and was motivated to start a movement called, the "St. Louis Prayer Project" where she encourages others to pray on a daily basis for today's youth.

As an Entrepreneur, Tonita uses the platform to engage in her passion for fashion, exercise, and natural hair tips while mentoring young ladies. She is the co-owner of Fashion Remix Online Boutique, which specializes in statement jewelry and accessories.

She is also a full time nurse and has found the time to share her personal experiences in hopes of inspiring others to make small changes that could lead to life changing rewards.

Simply put, Tonita loves teaching others to pray, have compassion for others, exercise, and of course activate "Shut-up grace" in their everyday lives.

If you would like to stay in touch with Tonita Smith, go to www.AuthorTonitaSmith.com.

Use the pages below to pen down your thoughts about the seven principles

---

Made in the USA
San Bernardino, CA
21 March 2016